Book III......
Conundrum En passant

Book III......
Conundrum En passant

poems by

Thomas Walker

Thomas Walker Publications
Eagle River, Alaska

Book III......Conundrum En passant

Cover Photo: A desert landscape at dusk with the sand marked out
in a dark and light checkered chess board pattern by Allan Swart
License Terms: http://www.123rf.com/license.php?type=standard

Library of Congress Control Number: 2013903640
ISBN 978-0615775531

Thomas Walker Publications
Eagle River, Alaska
www.thomas-walker-institute.com

Email: contact@thomas-walker-institute.com

To
every poem
I left chained to a tree
in the backyard of my mind.

the mystery of the missing,

Contents

Calliope Has Come My Way 1

I shook my head, and everything else was arranged 2

Telephone Line 3

It's Not Out There..4

Part of the Whole 5

It Won't Be Long Now..6

Go ahead, believe it......I don't care...7

Up in the Loft...8

My Wife...9

Canyon Winds 10

The Bride Killer 11

Every Last Drop of It...12

Green Fields of Rain 13

The Pig That Got Away 14

Night in the Prairie..15

Somewhere 16

The Poet Who Sighed..18

Amoral Love...20

Very, Very, Ordinary...21

The Masked Weaver...22

Kiss the Fire 24

Entomologist Glasses 25

Just for a While 26

Dying 27

The Cryptic Poet's Sea 28

The Value of Your Laughter 29

The One 30

The Miserable Contemplator 31

Blue Rabbits 32

The Slow Road 33

Deep Within 36

Freedom 37

Señorita You're in Trouble Again 38

The Tragedy 40

F??? 41

Or 42

Necro Insider 43

Hell's Moat 44

Drinking Rain 45

The Anointed Town 46

my life 48

Finding Nevermore 49

Plasticity Uprising 50

The Fire-eating Mole 51

Genie in the Bottle 52

I Hope to See You Soon 53

Here Today, Here to Stay 54

Orangutan Thought 55

After the Fire 56

I'll See You Tomorrow 57

One Step Closer...58

Fiddle About 60

Nanosecond..61

Success...62

Sitting on the Porch 63

Lost Gypsy Grand Finale 64

Take Me There..65

One Night in Caldera..66

Highway 5 (a day in the life of a leather tramp)...............67

Doom 68

The Story Has Begun..70

I'd Take You Everywhere 71

Having You Near...72

Small Town Girl 73

Last Thoughts of an Ordinary Night (a fragment that should
perhaps be revised) and A Title that Should Perhaps Be Shortened
(but then again would it really be the same) and Yes, That is a
Question So Here's Your Damn QUESTION MARK - ? (.)...........74

Coming Home...75

One for Emily 76

One More Night of Misery 77

Billions of Dreams..78

Indian Blanket 79

One Night in Juarez..80

Passing Through Cowboy Country 82

The Lonely Outlaw...83

The Devil's Sound 84

The Thanator...86

With a Knife 87

The Virgin Dreamer...88

Poor Boy 90

Without Hesitation 91

Out of the Swamp 92

The Brightest Stars 93

Pirate Lunacy..94

Springtime in the Mourning Mountains........................96

Delicate Geometry 98

I Howl for You (a coyote prayer).....................................99

Mutiny Anticipation 100

Warm Sand 102

In the City...103

Mississippi Queen..104

Temporary Direction 105

Driving to the Woods...106

The Vacancy..107

The Beginning...108

Book III......
Conundrum En passant

Calliope Has Come My Way

Because you say
my words
don't mean,

a goddamned thing
to you;
to you,
I'm going to write

a little song
to prove
that there is light,
to prove
that it's in sight,
to prove
that it's not you,
to prove
that it's not true.

Not true.
Not true.

Prove that it's not true.

I shook my head, and everything else was arranged

The feast of friends,
the glimmering signs
on the side of the road.

It all depends
on which side
of the road you're on,
whether or not
you understand
the thoughts and dreams
of carnivorous flowers;
the flesh-eating powers
in my garden
.....oh, pardon
.....oh, pardon.

Telephone Line

I see a tree
standing next to a tree;
one is deeply rooted,
one is 22906-B.
The similarities
are only there
for the few
that can see;
below the truth
underlies reality.

It's Not Out There

I walk this lonely ball of fire,
yet I am so far from alone.
I've herds of friends
but only......out there.
And so, on my own
I'm off to wander;
dragging the bone
I walk and ponder.

But no matter how far I dredge,
and how long I plunder;
the pyramids of life are always close by;
liquid madness, pouring thunder.

Is there really such a thing as loneliness?
asks the saturated, sanguine sky.
To yourself, I will tell you this,
Thou shall not contemplate on such a lie.

You know you'll always have a friend
if you just penetrate your mind.
Although it may not be what you're looking for,
the meaning of anything, you will find.

Always remember
that the road to nowhere,
never misleads.

Part of the Whole

I have to disperse
the learned burden
bundled and trundled
inside my head.
If I don't rid of it soon,
I will surely wind up dead;
upon which
I will forever cease
to be that
all important piece.

To have my body frozen
in time
and rocketed
into space;
to become
a representation
of man
and not a face;
to find meaning
in life,
not just
a sense of place;
to be discovered
as a great
part of
an interwoven lace.

It Won't Be Long Now

I left home just a week before
searching for something inside.
After twenty-some years of spinning around,
it was time to get off of the ride.
So I headed out for the great north woods
leaving your world behind;
had to get rid of all the things
that cluttered up my mind.
I wrote to my family one last time,
said, "I just had to get away."
Especially told my best girl,
we'd meet again someday......
if it was meant to be.....
floating through an endless sea.

Now I'm walking down the brick road of fate;
if I don't get off soon I'll die.
Sometimes you have to do what you want
and quit being life's alibi.
So I'm stepping off of this beaten path.
Who knows where I'll go?
But whatever's out there, I'm telling you,
I've just gotta know!
Now leaves are blowin' into my face,
sand is filling up my shoes,
and the only thing I have left to do
is to keep trying not to lose......
my sanity.....
floating through this endless sea.

Go ahead, believe it......I don't care

All I want
is a little thinkin';
get something done
before we start sinkin'.

Can't you see it's time
to find out why.....
everything we seem to do
always comes back
tumblin' through
mirrors in the sky.....

What's the use
in tryin' anyway?
I could sit here
and write all day.
You'll find out,
the earth really isn't round;
someday,
with your back to the ground.

But let me tell you,
you have nothing to fear;
gold and diamonds
whisper in your ear.....

Up in the Loft

.....and the evil wicked way
I roll around in hay
hating everybody,
but loving you today.

Pumping milk merrily
with each pleasant pounding thrust.
I have to say, 'I wish I may'.
I have to say, 'I wish I must'.
And fill your hollow soul
with happiness,
simple joy, and lust.

My Wife

She is my wife.
She is my life.
She is the knife
that cuts and twists.
She is the heart that bleeds,
the one that feeds
the wolves of my soul.

Canyon Winds

Come on, babe.
Step a little bit closer to the edge, babe.
Close your eyes....
close your eyes....

let the winds go
rushing....
rushing....
through your long dark hair,
and up and down your soul;
making the sweet sound
of loving you.

Come on, babe.
Step a little bit closer to the edge, babe.
Close your eyes....
close your eyes....

lean your head back
reaching....
reaching....
up toward the darkened sky,
and up and down your soul;
listen to the canyon winds
making sweet love to you.

The Bride Killer

A little blood and misunderstanding;
she misunderstood my needs.....
all the greed's
of a murdering madman.

Ancient heat,
the sweltering pain;
a cool terrain
for lizards and wasps,
scorpions and snakes.
No oceans, no seas.
No rivers, no lakes.

A refuge for a poet or martyr;
or perhaps just a killer,
lost and unknown.
A place for souls to beg and barter
with life and death;
where all are alone.

With thoughts of darkness,
and somber isolation;
eyes upon stars,
a distant migration
to remind us of smallness,
to do as you please,
and to do whatever it takes
to put you at ease.

Time to roll off,
head to the next town,
and plunder the whiteness
of another wedding gown.

Every Last Drop of It

Eat the meal of Eden.
LUSTING
(THRUSTING)
every nice, shiny Red Apple
you can get a hold of.
SHOVING
(LOVING)
snakes and venom
to the very light
and sight of Womb,
(the tomb of my soul)
the goal
of existence;
every last d

              r   o

                 p

           o   f

              i

               t

              .

Green Fields of Rain

Some girls are pensive,
their heads in the clouds.
Oh, some girls are high!
Some girls down low,
covered with shrouds.
Oh, some girls can't fly!

Some girls make motions
of colors and swirl.
Some girls remind me of floating away.
Some girls, as still as oceans beneath.
Some girls remind me of wanting to stay.

But she's got heartache and she's got pain;
a girl on the brink of going insane.
Weaving her way through rugged terrain;
never to feel ever again.

Tell her you love her
when fields are green,
but never make a promise you cannot keep.
Forget where you're going,
remember where you've been,
and hold her in your arms as she falls asleep.

Wake up with the rhythm of rain;
the song of an old tin roof.

The Pig That Got Away

This is the story of the pig that lived all alone,
far away from the town he once called his home.
He escaped from the farm; it was a long time ago,
with nowhere to run and nowhere to go.

On the banks of the river while playing his flute,
an owl appeared and gave him a hoot.
Just what are you doing, I bid you fair warning,
playing that flute at three in the morning?

I'm sorry to inform you, I'm sorry to say,
that I came out here just so I could play.
For back on the farm it was work and then sleep;
lying around in the mud so deep.

Too much work to be done and never too soon,
so I came out here to write songs with the moon.
Now I play when I want and I play all night,
until the moon slowly fades…. and drifts out of sight.

You see that is why I choose to live out here,
where I can wake up each day, tranquility near.
Where I can walk down to the river, just my flute and me;
with freedom, solitude, and serenity.

So he picked up his flute and began to play,
calmly astute as he walked away.
"No more will I wallow," the pig played loudly.
"Because I got away," the pig played proudly.

Night in the Prairie

Where were you when I was cryin'?
Where were you when I was lyin'
flat on my back in the middle of the prairie?

At 3:00 A.M. life can be scary
when the wind hides the cars;
when the fog hides the stars.

You're all alone.
You're all alone.

You never loved me for who I was.
You never loved me, just because,
I wouldn't give up on my dreams.

At 3:00 A.M. you can hear the screams
when people are giving up hope;
when people are learning to cope

with being alone,
with being alone.

Somewhere

With your back against the wall
at least she knows you are there.
Somewhere;
somewhere out there
on the road to eternity.

For what we observe is limited
to what we expect to see;
within the range of senses,
or where technology

has extended our powers
and advanced our ability,
to go somewhere else
on the road to eternity.

So, take a deep breath.
End the universe as we know it
and show it.
After all,
the best place to hide something
is right in front of your face.

And the microscope is worthy
not in its ability to enlarge,
but in its ability to separate;
separate somewhere
from somewhere
on the road to eternity.

Like aimless dead wanderers,
through the void,
roaming at random;
they are delicate souls
traveling in tandem.

A camera could record these trails
for posterity.
However,
time is continuously overflowing,
and mysteriously unknowing;
as is the story of the blue moon.

Oh know,
.....I think I just lost a proton.

The Poet Who Sighed

And when she died,
she finally got to meet the wise man.
Was it God, or was it just a poet who sighed?

.....well, the poet sighed and said, "Oh darling,
it's just great of you to join me here.
Is there anything that you'd like to know?"

.....the lady cried and said, "You know, I cry
in the sunshine and I cry in the rain.
Can you tell me why I cry, why do I always cry?"

.....the poet sighed and said, "You know,
a lot of people cry, a lot of people try,
and everybody has to die."

.....she stopped crying and said to the poet,
"I'm really glad to be here with you.
Is there anything you would like to know?"

.....the poet sighed and said, "Hey, some people cry
and some people sigh. It's a twist in a strange world;
so you just go ahead and cry.

.....so she cried to the poet, "I tell ya,
it's really sad to be here with you but
is there anything that you'd like to know?"

.....the poet sighed and said, "Sure, I try
to help and I try to be the wise man; can you
tell me why I try? Why do I even try?"

.....the lady cried and said, "Ah yes, you see
it's not in being right, and it's not in being wrong.
It's what you think, that's all! That is why you try."

.....so the poet sighed and said, "It is
really great of you to join me here!
Is there anything else that you'd like to know?"

.....the lady cried, "One more thing.
I live my life and then I die, can you tell me
why I die? Oh, why do I have to die?"

.....well the poet sighed and said, "When you die,
you get to meet the wise man. It may be God,
or it may just be a poet who sighs."

.....the lady cried and said, "Hey, some people sigh
and some people die. It's a twist in a strange world;
so you just go ahead and sigh."

Amoral Love

She was taken
by the serpent's rise;
another tulip in disguise.
Dark and deep unto his eyes,
the eyes of amoral love.

Now those who question their times so bleak,
will never find it while they seek.
So live your pain, live it tough,
and when you've suffered long enough,
that is when the serpent comes

```
   l i          n g  t h            o u          l   a                r t
 s      t    r i          r o      y    r        u          n          a
     h   e                u g h            s  o          d   h   e
```

and stays until you're torn apar
                              t.

Book III......Conundrum En passant

Very, Very, Ordinary

Give me something I can hold.
How 'bout something made of gold?
Don't you know, you can be like me;
tie yourself down, then wish you were free.
All you need to do is go to school,
and get a job; it's the golden rule.
Don't you know, you can be like me;
buy a pet and rape a tree.
Now your life is almost through;
your children on the same path too
Don't you know, you can be like me;
write your will and pay your fee.

21

Thomas Walker

The Masked Weaver

Architecture is in turmoil between
art as feeling,
and engineering as practicality.
A falsity has been created,
kind of like a breast implant;
it seems so real from the surface
but inside it is a canard,
a substitute for natural growth.

There is no growth.
There is no seed.
The seed must be found
before it can be planted.

Poetry is the most influential form
of communicating a 'mind'
to a public.

time - relation
life - ideas

Something must be done with the written word,
and like the wizard's magic spell
it must look to the core.

mind - people
expression - feeling

That is where a genesis occurs.
Genesis......
do you know what I mean?

Harvard,
Yale,
Princeton......

you bound man's capacities.
Your teachers preach their religion
as the missionary preaches his.

You shake your heads so sarcastically
as you tell us what not to be,
and how we are supposed to see
the world.

Thank your God
for people like me.
After all,
the masked weaver
needs only practice.

Kiss the Fire

Candle, candle, burning bright;
twist my words all through the night.

For if my time should be tomorrow,
or perhaps......the next;
upon this paper, my mind reflects.

When your life flows and flows
through the fingers of reality,
this expectation......is mere fallacy.

So kiss the fire, fear not its burn;
all you can feel, is that which you learn.

Come with me to the other side,
to the forbidden world
where madness can reside;
in your heart, in your soul,
in paper and pen,
bleeding and bleeding, again and again.

No longer need you clench fists of rage;
this is no land where wars are wage.

If you care to stay you need not pay rent;
this is no place where time is spent.

Entomologist Glasses

Upon the roach
you cast
a thoughtless label.
Morbid and vile,
such wretched creatures.

But, my! Oh, my!
If you were
only able
to see beyond
it's surface features.

Just for a While

Everybody keeps telling me
that there's nothing in this world worth living for.
But now that I've found you,
I think I'll stick around you;
(for a while)
(for a while)
and maybe, just maybe, you won't hound me
with the typical miseries that surround me.
(for a while)
(for a while)
If the good and the bad were equal,
there would be no more people.
(for a while)
(for a while)
(just for a while)
The war, the hate, the violence, and the sex;
were not these in the days of tyrannosaurus rex?
And a son home for the weekend tosses his dad a ball
and says, "You know, things really haven't changed at all."
In the corner of a city, I ran into a friend;
she had three kids but never been a wife.
I kindly asked, what in the world
have you done with your life?
She said, "Why I make babies;
what else is there to do?"
So I gave a brief smile
and thought maybe it's true,
that humans today are truly deranged.
But honestly, have things ever really changed?

Dying

The dream poets do not exist
for poets do not dream
and life does not go on.
Is it beautiful to be remembered,
disillusioned
and numb?
My heart is like a balloon
filled with anger
and sadness.
All the while, slowly leaking,
my love escapes;
my life escapes.

The Cryptic Poet's Sea

You'll tell me my words
are just so absurd.
Where is my sunshine?

And that what's in my head
is better unsaid.
What are you giving?

So I'll crawl to the sea,
no one but me;
me on the inside.

Then I'll tell you I'm free,
free to be me;
no one to act like.

And this is where I would like to be;
in the darkest depths of the raging sea.
And this is where I would like to stay;
creating messages every day.
And this is where I would like to die;
ask me how, but do not ask me why.

The Value of Your Laughter

So long ago, but not too long ago,
I came across an old picture.
We seemed to be so insecure;
our love was real, but not so pure

So long ago, so long ago,
we crossed the golden sand,
through the valley hand in hand;
searching for our promised land.

So long ago, so long ago,
we had our days of diligence,
our days of confidence,
our days of immense.....happiness.

So long ago, where did it go?
But now that it's gone and past,
I've come to see at last,
the value of your laughter.

The One

When your life is like rain and the wind doesn't blow;
you've got no one to talk to…..you've got nowhere to go.
Just look for the lady, the one with the glow;
for she is the sunshine…..that in your heart does flow.
And when you find her, let your emotions show,
or right through your fingers…..she will swiftly go.
Just ask for her help in climbing out of the abyss,
and when she lifts you up…..you must tell her this:

There are many things in life that I can do without,
but without you…..I would just drift about;
under the lonely lovers' rainbow, where stricken hearts do stroll,
waiting for misery's spell…..to take its toll.
For when my ship is sinking and I wish that I did not exist,
you are always there for me…..there to assist.
You reach down to pull me out and if I refuse to come, you insist.
This is why you are the one…..the one I cannot resist.

The Miserable Contemplator

I was silently sitting
beneath the willow tree
when a smiling young girl
came dancing to me.

She said, why must you sit here
looking so sad?

I said, why must you come here
looking so glad?

Silence......(no more smile)

Little darling, you see,
you are quite different;
different than me.

Wherever you go,
joy and happiness
are sure to follow.

Wherever I go,
there will always be
misery and sorrow

So go,
(with your smile)
and
let me be me.

Blue Rabbits

Your erotic spiritual force,
reckless and crashing,
throws me off course.

The lost tracks buried beneath
the hot desert sand;
I do hereby bequeath

that the last thought is true,
from the heart,
with a touch of blue.

It's too late honey, to turn back now.
You've wandered into my land;
let's not forget how.

Give in to me, love penetrates soon.
Swallow my pride on a sunny afternoon;
upon the next road
with your lips against mine.

The rabbits of blue
will whisper to you,
no fears,
no fears,
if yesterday brings tears
rolling down your cheeks in pain.
For how can we measure the sunniest days
without the days of rain.

The Slow Road

Wine, Women, and Paradise;
jewels of the wicked nest
conspiring with misfortune,
and throwing pebbles into the eyes
of a dragon sleeping in the meadow.
I don't know what went wrong.
I just got high one day,
way high;
fuck everybody nestling in pleasure.
I'll say it again,
fuck everybody nestling in pleasure;
any form of education.
Fuck the oak tree,
sweet mother oak
forlorn nobility.
Speak in daffodil rhymes.
What could you possibly do without?

If the doors of perception were cleansed,
and the answer was simply
that the sum of all consequences
is zero (absolute)?
Now we're entering the planet's surface,
it's almost an impenetrable mist.
The thunder was cracking like a sonic boom.
The lightning was heartless,
destroying every weeping willow;
there was a girl right behind
quietly screaming.
The storm was closing in fast, she had to take cover,
but her lover…..just kept walking through.
I gave a razor blade to a good friend of mine;
no more walking down the line.
My expected insanity……
sometimes I feel dizzy/ cut myself/

see me bleeding/ my blood is black/
I've got to get my baby back.

My blood is black.

You thought it was just a game.
You thought I was asleep,
but you kept on playing,
and now you're in too deep......
now you're in too deep.
Confessions of loneliness, pictures of a dream;
thought of you as a whore,
thought of you as a queen,
but now you're at the crossroads
of something in between......
something in between
Cut myself/ see me bleeding/
my blood is gray;
(gone) finale.

Some of us are losers
right out of the gate.
Some of us will never heed way to a king,
but it is plain to see that I am
one hundred percent misery.
Some of us run in circles,
though always out in front.
Some of us never learn to run with the hunt.
Passion flips the night on and off
like a light switch.
The madam says,
you'll never make it......you know,
with those feelings inside your head,
because.....
because eventually you'll end up dead.

Well tell her that I use to love her,
but now that she doesn't need me around;
a new lady I have found.

Maybe it's another battle gone awry
or just something we call time,
but I can't seem to get you,
never going to let you......
get you off of my mind.

Sometimes I wish that someone
would put a bullet through my brain.
Sleeping in the rain
in hopes that I would
never wake again,
see me bleeding/ my blood is gone
gone.....gone (finale).

Deep Within

I lost my mind but found my heart,
just in time to play the part;
the part of hope,
the part of giving,
the part of living out a dream.
I lost my house but I found my home,
somewhere near a place called Nome.
I lost my life but I found a wife.
It's a long forgotten, broken story
about wind and rain, love and pain,
and the quest for sacred glory.

I made it in without a scratch,
looked around and released the hatch.

In the death and the vile and the putrid smell;
the darkest depths will surely tell.
My love reins strong and true,
among the fiery pits of hell.
And you say that this is a tragedy,
but it does not appear that way to me.
For anyone who feels love like that,
it cannot be......
it cannot be......
look at me......
it can
not
be.

Freedom

Freedom is
a sacrifice
that few will
ever make.
Like a caged dog
being fed;
refusing......
to run away,
refusing......
to be free,
choosing......
instead,
to serve.

Señorita You're in Trouble Again

I've had that funny feeling inside ever since I met you.
Fluctuations seem to happen naturally
and someday I know that you'll have to leave,
but there is nothing wrong with being free.
There is nothing wrong with being free.

Running around looking for the answer;
the answer that no one else can see.
Trying to find a hole that you can die in;
Señorita, you've turned out a lot like me.

Everybody's got to ride the freight train sometime;
straight through the sun with felicity.
Love is (is not) the answer and you know it.
Señorita, you've turned out a lot like me.

Sleeping naked down by the ocean;
looking up to make your last plea.
Is there anything out there that can bring me passion?
Señorita, you've turned out a lot like me.

Flowers never grow outside your window;
living in darkness is simplicity.
You've learned to accept all of the misfortune.
Señorita, you've turned out a lot like me.

Maybe in some far off land you'll sit and wonder
whether or not your love was meant to be,
or if he, or she, or they will be forgotten.
Señorita, you've turned out a lot like me.

Living on the edge has gotten you noticed,
but you've never even seen your sanity.
Surrounded by the act of desperation;
Señorita, you've turned out a lot like me.

When you're living outside the circle, you must remember
that you have no friends or no company,
but that doesn't bother you much the same.
Señorita, you've turned out a lot like me.

The Tragedy

Tragedy provokes emotion and
Emotion is a very human thing.
It moves us, it tears us,
and it excites us all.

That is why it is old,
......Australopithecus.
That is why it is popular,
......Shakespeare.
That is why we lie
......a true lady.
That is why we kill
......a true poet.

F???

I was just eighteen, a blues machine
taking a walk in the dark.
When along comes a girl of pitch black curl,
and says, what are you doing here?
I said, I hate to intrude but I'm feeling lewd;
do you think you could spark my dreams?

I listened and I heard,
I listened and I heard.

I listened and I heard,
I listened and I heard.

I listened and I heard,
I listened and I heard.

I listened and I heard,
I listened and I heard.

Or

I'm going to wherever, to do whatever I please.
I'm going to wherever, to do whatever I please.

Talk about a ramblin'......
talk about a travelin'......
talk about the way I want to be.

I watch the weeks go by
like waves on a shore.
Such is the life
of a fool with nowhere to go.
Feelin' low now.....
feelin' low now......
I don't care about much anymore.
Watchin' the sun sail on.....
sail on by......
sail on by like a song.

Like a song of insane love
and rain......
rain......
rain......
early morning rain.
Please don't forget the sun
and all the love......
all of the love and pain.
The two together
make the sun and rain,
and all the flowers of the mind.

Necro Insider

Blood dripping,
frothing......
it doesn't last for long, but
I get the need to kill.
Spill the blood, everybody should
get crazy one time.
The serenity of my wicked insanity.
I am a zombie now,
another one of the walking dead.
I feel as though I am no longer living.
I don't even know if I'm in here anymore.
I don't even know if I exist.
I can hardly even move.
I can hardly even breathe.
I just see blurry images go by.

Thomas Walker

Hell's Moat

Another song I could not write,
another dark and lonely night.
I cannot see a sign of light
at the end of the tunnel;
funneling my dreams
through life's endless rivers and streams,
filled with the blood and the howling screams
of lost and broken souls.
All along, I sit here in my jungle boat
Desperately trying to keep afloat.
If I can only get across the moat,
the moat that surrounds the darkest depth.

I'm going insane.
I'm losing my mind.
Ha hah ha ha......
I'm going fucking crazy,
everything is so hazy
with a violet breeze,
fire and freeze,
and brittle dead trees.

Is it just me......
wanting so badly just to break free,
free from the pain of life's daily dungeon.

Drinking Rain

And the black bird
sits on the side of the road,
stares at me growing old,
and drinking rain.

And the black bird
hears the dying chimes,
of the busted rhymes
in the graveyard of lonely dreams.

And the black bird
sings in broken harmony.
"what will be will be,"
and flies away.

And the old man,
he watches the skies,
a deathly look in his eyes,
and drinking rain.

Thomas Walker

The Anointed Town

There once was a little town in a land so serene,
with skies so blue and grass so green.
…..not a hurry,
…..no need to worry,
peace and tranquility ruled the way
in this land of no work;
in this land of all play.

For these people were livin'
with everything given;
given on a silvery platter.
Nothing seemed to matter,
their lives were so routine
like sheep in the pasture;
like a clockwork machine.

Until down from the rivers
with their arrows and their quivers;
the rats came marching in one lazy afternoon,
dancing with a pig to his favorite tune.

The townspeople cringed
at the sound and the sight,
shocked and stunned
by their current plight.
They despised this pig,
and thought less of his friends.
How you feel about it?
Well, that all depends.

Was the town falling apart?
Was it losing its heart?
Had the rats overtaken?
Was joy forsaken?

Well, the pig picked up his flute, calmly astute,
and began to play his tune of the day,
"you can't always get what you want....."
The rats would follow, wail and wallow,
"find us a new place to haunt."

And so the piper moved on after making his point;
off to the next town that he would anoint.
You see, the rats may be down, but surely not out.
They will always find a place to scurry about.
Scurry about.
Scurry about.

my life

I'm so bored, I'm so fucking bored.
I can hardly even think,
my skull is on the brink.
It hurts so fucking bad
I can hardly even think.
My motivation is an ancient memory,
a last chance effort to dig something
out of the corner of my mind;
to find the energy to be
to be anything at all.
A lump of clay, a pile of shit,
piss and vomit.
Miles of it.
Miles of it.
Miles and miles and miles of it,
a never ending tunnel of it.
Piles of shit.
Piles of shit.
Piles and piles and piles of it,
floating in piss and vomit.
Piss and vomit
everywhere,
miles of it.
A never ending tunnel of it
and I have had it, but yet I go on,
and on and on,
and on and on;
through miles of shit,
through piles of shit,
endless, endless miles of it.
Shit,
piss,
and
vomit.

Finding Nevermore

I sit and rock;
my eyes are closed.
I hear my heart,
and it imposed......

I'm so fucking bored.
I'm bored to death,
to hatred and vile
with every breath.

I'm always alone,
and close to death;
every waking hour,
every miserable breath.

Plasticity Uprising

The world is old,
it has made its gold;
placed all its bets,
and had to fold.
Wasted all its breath
in lands so cold,
until all that was left
was a plastic mold,
a plastic mold of a vagina.

The Fire-eating Mole

At the deepest darkest depth,
in the deepest darkest corner
of the deepest darkest hole,
lived the deepest darkest creature,
a creature without a soul.

/////

In the dark and misty morning, down we went;
down and down and down and down.

/////

It seems like only yesterday
that pain was here to stay,

but I don't want to die now;
I've forgotten how to cry now.

I know that it's been said many times before,
of this I'm very sure,

'One and one doesn't always make two!'
You know that it's true; it's oh so true.

Blue and blue make blue;
yes they do, babe, yes they do.

Like fire and fire make burning desire,
and that is why......I love you!

Genie in the Bottle

Don't let your dreams curl up in the corner and die.
Die with a room full of dreams.
Dream with a room full of dying pain.

You're always having fun down there,
at the bottom of the bottle.
Girl, it's time to take a hard look at me.

Everything looks different in black and white;
you see things more clearly......just a little bit of light.
In the darkness of the night,
such a wonderful sight.....to see.
For the spring and the summer,
with their elegant color,
make us forget what is real.

Dreams don't come true,
when the sky is blue.
Dreams don't come true......
or they would not be dreams!

I Hope to See You Soon

Another night of darkness.
Another day of sunlight.
Another chance to find love.
Another chance to lose it.

And I think that love is just a reason,
a reason to forget.
Forget the pain around you.
Forget the world is falling.

And I think that love is just a reason,
a reason to linger;
a reason to survive.

I hope to see you soon.

Thomas Walker

Here Today, Here to Stay

With it, realms of certainty and euphoria.
Without it, the world ending.
With it, the world is slowing — no more, no worse.
Without it, we can make a world in our own minds,
and inhabit it with doubts and frustrations.
With it, we can make a world in our own minds,
and inhabit it with optimism and hope.

When you came to me,
I could tell that you needed to run free,
and it was time to fly away.
Fly awaaaaaay, fly awaaaaaay.
And then the love in disguise,
in the back of your darkened eyes,
appeared like a sunrise in the sky.
In the skyyyyyyy, in the skyyyyyyy.

I'd rather be nobody with you,
than some somebody with her.
I'd rather be uncertain with you,
than be with some someone for sure.
I'd rather be all mixed up with you,
than be with some somebody that's pure.
I'd rather be in love with you,
than having to endure......
a life without you by my side.

It came to me.
like an orchestrated symphony
in disguise.
I knew I was here to stay,
on a 5th floor balcony;
the sun shining free
in your eyes.

Orangutan Thought

I feel like an orangutan
in a cage.
Somebody throw me
a bowling ball.
I'm so fucking bored.
Come on over here......
I'll smash your little skull,
just for fun.

After the Fire

I met death,
and it laughed without a smile.
But I shook my head,
and laughed back
with a smile none the less.
Even death bores me these days,
but what can you do.
I guess it's that tangled web we weave thing.

In the long dark hours when
frozen time lurks,
and the dungeon door slams shut.
The gore becomes frighteningly obvious,
and looking back there is no door.....no more.
Now, forward forlorn all hopes,
and forward is the only choice.
Well.....one of two, anyway.
Curiosity kills mightily,
and lack of.....kills painfully;
and disdainfully moving on,
we forage every vile corner
in search of something useful,
in search of something necessary.

I'll See You Tomorrow

I think I need a female companion
because it's pretty sad when your girl
has to try and make conversation with you
by asking about a football game
that she could not care less about.
It's pretty fucking sad.

I think I need a female companion.
Someone I could spend my lunch hour with.
A soft and silky voice,
A tender and delicate ear.

I think I need a female companion.
I'll see you tomorrow, my dear.

Thomas Walker

One Step Closer

Boxcar song......take me home,
with the weeds, forever to roam.
Across the prairies, all night long,
to the mountains where I belong.
With a sad hearted role,
and a mad hearted soul;
searching for redemption,
searching for the mole.

All aboard the 1109.
Don't bring anything at all, just grab a sign.
'Fuck You, Too!'
and go to the end of the line.
Get one step closer to being unborn.
You think you know what you know.
I think I'm ready......ready to go.

You, you were my nova cane.
When I felt I was going insane,
you were my nova cane.
Yes you, you numbed the pain.
You were my nova cane.

When I was with you girl,
nothing really mattered.
When I was with you girl,
the glass earth shattered.
When I was with you girl,
I was free, yeah, oh yeah
I was free, and nothing really mattered.

Now I am alone again.
Now I am on my own.
My soul has been amputated,
my love and my life have been sedated.

What have I become?
Gelatin......a shapeless mold.
Globular nothingness.
That is what I am;
globular nothingness.
And I hate and I hate and I hate.
I hate everything, even hate.
I hate everything and everyone around;
everything lost and everything found.

When I look into the mirror, I see a ghost.
A ghost of a man knowing
that being alive is not enough.
Going to his grave knowing
that he has lived, that is something,
that is really something.
Something, more than life itself.

Oh yes, I'll say it again
as many times as I have to.
Being alive and living are two different things;
like being a bird, and a bird without wings.

Thomas Walker

Fiddle About

Wow, it's pretty amazing down here.
Way down here.
No, a little bit further.
No, a little bit further.
That's it, way down here.

I think I need a female companion
to throw me a rope,
to let down her hair like Rapunzel,
her long and beautiful hair.
Help me find my way out of here.
Help me dear.
Wrap your soul around my skin,
lift me up and out.

I think I need a female companion
someone to fiddle about,
fiddle about, fiddle about.

Nanosecond

I think I'll take
a nanosecond
out of my
left hemorrhaging brain,
flick a switch,
and vomit up
the last six months
of pain,
and let all those
wasted memories
wash right down
the drain.

Success

I think success
is giving yourself
the time to do those things
that you enjoy the most.

But I guess some people
don't know how......
to enjoy,
so they end up being failures.

Sitting on the Porch

I live with fourteen thousand
million billion fools;
build some more temples,
build some more schools.
You can teach them how
to read your god's word,
but you can't teach them to think.

You can keep searching,
and searching,
and searching,
for that missing link.
I'll just sit here
on my porch watching,
and have another drink.

Thomas Walker

Lost Gypsy Grand Finale

The world is violently spinning around,
but I sure can't tell,
lying here with you girl;
my hand caressing the mound
between your lovely, lovely legs.
I think I know what is real.

You are my French silk maid,
a sunny Sunday treat;
breakfast in bed girl,
you taste so sweet.

You are my farmer girl,
rolling around in the hay;
my hot American pie
in the back of a Chevrolet.

You are my bikini girl
on the shores of Rio;
bringing your friend
to make it a trio.

You are my lost gypsy,
the grand finale,
my cabin mistress,
for a weekend in Denali.

Take Me There

Do you ever
notice
how the ice,
the blustering
coldness
numbs the pain
of
every
thing.

If
it gets cold enough
then
nothing exists.
Nothing,
not even pain.
Nothing exists
at absolute zero.
All molecular motion
ceases to exist.

A thought,
a memory,
has to contain
molecular motion
in order to occur.

One Night in Caldera

Wake up sunrise,
my girl,
the gathering draws near.
The nearest burning desire
still there, after all the fire.

One white hot night
in Caldera.

Light cotton,
fluttering in the steamy breeze,
like a butterfly
in the bedroom balcony of my eye.
A tear for the lasting ideals of romanticism.

I'd be the happiest man on earth.

Highway 5 (a day in the life of a leather tramp)

Hey, it's a brand new day.
Hey, it's a brand new day.
Hey, it's a brand new day.
Hey, it's a brand new day.

Today, the sun won't go away.
Today, the morning is here to stay.
Today is a lifelong holiday.
Today, walking down the coastal highway.

Today, my mind put at ease.
Today, no idiosyncrasies.
Today, I leave a path behind.
Today, the future begins to unwind.

Hey, there's nowhere to go today.
Hey, there's nowhere to go today.
Hey, there's nowhere to go today.
Hey, there's nowhere to go today.

Thomas Walker

Doom

She's got a piece of a broken down future,
she's got a piece of me.
She's got a window unit in the bedroom,
doooooom......she's got meeeee!
Doom, doom,
doom, doom.
doom, doom,
doom, dooooooom,
she's got meeeee!

She's got me, she's got me
moving very blindly
up and down the fatal highway.
She's got me, she's got me,
stars fluttering in the eyes
back and forth until decay.

She's got me, she's got me
from town to town to town;
in a world of going nowhere.
She's got me, she's got me
dreaming about the sunshine;
destiny, do beware.

She's got me, she's got me
looking at the present;
hair blowing in the breeze.
She's got me, she's got me
standing on the prairie,
as if, two lonely trees.

She's got me, she's got me
wondering about tomorrow;
if I'm going to stay here.

She's got me, she's got me
flying thru the window;
pain is drawing near.

She's got a piece of a broken down future,
she's got a piece of me.
She's got a window unit in the bedroom,
doooooom......she's got meeeee!
Doom, doom,
doom, doom.
doom, doom,
doom, dooooooom,
she's got meeeee!
oh yeah, she's got meeeee!

Thomas Walker

The Story Has Begun

I was walking down a rocky shore
when I came upon the silver door.
I knew, somehow;
somehow......I just knew
that I'd been here once before.

I could tell by the loud and constant hum,
the gentle pounding of a drum,
and the distant hollow guitar strum.
I could tell.....something truly unique
was dwindling upon my
heart like a streak.
A far and distant streak of lightning

This silver door I'd seen before.
A different place,
a different time,
and locked it does remain.
A knock and a bang, a shoulder and a kick,
but this time I'm prepared
with a dynamite stick.
A blast so loud and then clearing smoke,
an ominous figure in a hooded cloak
looking in disbelief, he started to run.
Through the door I chased,
and thus, the story has begun.

I'd Take You Everywhere

If I was the last living soul on earth;
in my right front pocket
I'd carry a picture of you
in a silver watch and locket.

I'd take you down into the Grand Canyon;
with that smile in your eyes
we'd awake side by side,
and watch the morning sun rise.

I'd sail you around the Ring of Fire
in dire need of glowing explosion;
your heart still alive in tune with my beat
immune to life's corrosion.

I'd take you to Mount Everest's peak,
hold you mighty above my head
and spin around and spin around,
until we both were dead.

Thomas Walker

Having You Near

We live in a world
where little is certain.
Where truth hides......
behind a stained
glass curtain.

A world of resistance;
a world of doubt.
Forever the search......
to find
what it's all about.

Yet one thing is genuine,
one thing for sure.
My love for you,
relentless and pure!

Home is not home
when you're not around.
Having you near,
bliss is abound.

If heaven doesn't have us
side by side;
Then heaven's a place......
I'll never reside.

Small Town Girl

Small town girl I like the way you look at me.
I love the way you want to be
in your small town world
with your small town dreams.
It always seems, it always seems…..so free.
It always seems to be…..so free.

To take a barefoot midnight stroll,
to see your white dress shimmering.
In the moonlight by the lake,
a smile, one could never mistake
for anything less than eternity;
eternity in your lips and eyes.

Small town girl, come with me.
Down to the forgotten mystic diner;
we'll share a slice of fresh apple pie.
I'll tell you what I used to want.
I'll tell you what I used to need.
Before I met you, everything seemed to matter.

Sitting with you, sharing a swing
in the front yard of tomorrow land.
Watching the sun go down,
something in blue and orange happens
that no words could ever explain.
Your hair blowing in the wind, and nothing matters.

Small town girl I like the way you look at me.
I love the way you want to be
in your small town world
with your small town dreams.
It always seems, it always seems…..so free.
It always seems to be…..so free.

Last Thoughts of an Ordinary Night (a fragment that should perhaps be revised) and A Title that Should Perhaps Be Shortened (but then again would it really be the same) and Yes, That is a Question So Here's Your Damn QUESTION MARK - ? (.)

4:00 A.M., and I try to make myself write something;
yet, I cannot force the illness
and you know the illness that I write of;
the thoughts controlling the thoughts of time,
momentous and delightful,
filled with melancholic nightmarish episodes,
one to another to another to another to another to another,
the continuing saga of almost there, then slowly backwards
A little bit further......a little bit closer.
A little bit further......a little bit closer;
and somebody out there
perhaps trying to decipher the texturing of text,
the poetics of nonsensical.
We are all believers, no matter what we believe;
we are all believers of something,
we are all dreamers no matter what we dream,
we are all dreamers of something,
and like all believers and like all dreamers
we scorn and ridicule that which is not our own,
that which is not our way.
Face it, you are either one with me,
or no one at all,
no one at all,
no one at all.

No one at all.

Coming Home

I can't seem to find
anything......to ease my mind;
anything......but coming home to you.

Summer wind carry me,
carry me so far away.
Carry me away with the sunrise.
Follow me nighttime,
follow me with the morning.
Don't forget to leave me with today.
Today is the same, the same old story;
the never-ending glory......of love

Memories are near,
near to me......throughout the year;
a year of searching for lost freedom.
Searching leads me back,
back to where I started from;
rolling down the road, it seems so true.
I can't seem to find
anything......to ease my mind;
anything......but coming home to you.

I tried to make rain
wash away the road to you;
flooding the path from your heart to mine.
I can't seem to find
anything......to ease my mind;
anything......but coming home to you.
I'll be coming home;
coming home closer to you,
the closer I get to heaven.

One for Emily

Fire......
is the great prognosticator,
conqueror of all previous;
beginning of all ends,
end of all in its forefront.

Frozen......
cold death will
once again thaw out,
revealing those remnants
of preconceptions past.

Fire......
leaves but ashes,
ashes to erase all doubt;
doubt that you will be in my future,
doubt that I should see your smile.

One More Night of Misery

The good old, good old, good times;
again......they will never be.

You win some, you lose some,
so it has been said.
To make the anguish go away,
you'll have to behead.
What else, what else, what else can I do
for one more night of misery,
misery......with you.

One more fleeting inner light;
one more darkened, distant night.
One less lonely, lonely dream;
one last chance to redeem.
One more night, indigo blue,
one more night of misery with you.

The good old, good old, good times;
again......they will never be.

I could search low, low, and high
for something new and shiny, each day.
Or, I could walk in the clouds;
picking up pieces of frozen grey.
What else, what else, what else can I do
for one more night of misery,
misery......with you.

Give me one more night of misery;
one more night, tried and true.
I'll take one more night of misery;
one more night of misery with you.

Billions of Dreams

Billions of people;
billions of dreams.
I want to be this,
I want to be that,
I want to be......I just want to be.

Look at me, I'm afraid to die;
afraid of mortality.
I want to be,
I want to be something that will last.
I want to make this,
I want to make that.

Busy being afraid,
forgetting to live.
I have to do this, I have to do that
Billions of people;
billions of dreams.

But, I just want to be;
be left alone.
Please let me die in peace,
leave me alone.
I'm not afraid to die,
I just want to be.

Indian Blanket

Someone one told me
that if something is invisible,
and you cannot find it;
hold your arms out,
and it will come to you.

Now someone told you,
so open yourself wide.
I will be there;
I will come.

Thomas Walker

One Night in Juarez

The church of Christ is in neon;
the glamour girls are sniffing Freon.
The way they look at you, they must be on
......some godlike love.

Look at me on the one way road;
destination overload.
Now it's time to sing the ode
......to endless love.

Red, red rooms and a crystal ball;
naked eyed down every hall.
Don't close a door if you're afraid to fall
......deep in love.

Come with me,
sweet Marie.
Come with me,
insanity.
Come with me,
let's fall
......deep in love.

Long black hair and a silken dress;
what did you do to get in this mess?
Don't ever turn around unless
......you want love.

Come with me,
sweet Marie.
Come with me,
insanity.
Come with me,
let's undress
......you want love.

The signals are green but I have to stop;
the dogs run and the rabbits hop.
Lay your head back, it's time to drop
......this liquid love.

Come with me,
sweet Marie.
Come with me,
insanity.
Come with me,
and you'll get
......this liquid love.

The lights are getting stronger,
the radio looks longer,
and now it's time to conquer
......your true, true love.

Thomas Walker

Passing Through Cowboy Country

Through the crystal door
a goddess, not a whore.
A double shot of Jack Gloom,
then she takes you to her room.
Love is something she cannot comprehend,
but she has, oh so much, more to lend.
She'll take you in her arms;
credulous, lady-lust charms.

Sapphire......
is everything I've ever wanted.
She keeps my heart in line;
my money is her time.
Oh, Sapphire......
you mean everything to me.

She'll do anything she can
to make you feel like a man,
and I'd do anything I could
to make her feel just as good.
My passion has been seized;
I've never been so pleased.
If I ever make it back this way;
come again, the sacred lay.

Sapphire......
is everything I've ever wanted.
She keeps my heart in line;
my money is her time.
Oh, Sapphire......
you mean everything to me.

The Lonely Outlaw

After having robbed
dozens of banks and trains,
killing everything in my path;
I really am an outlaw now.
Lonely,
lonely;
I haven't got a home, I have no one,
I am always on the run.
Lonely
lonely;
nothing has ever worked out for me
except not getting caught, I suppose.
I've spent my whole live trying
to put a square peg into the round hole.
It is better to be miserable than
lonely,
lonely.
I have nothing, nothing at all;
no one to give to, no pride,
just pain, and hurting inside.
I feel like I am dying now.
I can see the goddess of death;
her snake eyes upon me,
lonely,
lonely.
It is only a matter of time before
someone shoots me in the back
for reward money.
I just want to get it over with;
I am old and ready to die.
I am just a scarred, ugly old man.
Lonely.
Lonely.

The Devil's Sound

I wonder if you-----remember me-----
like I, remember you-----

Every little thing / that we've ever done
is in my head-----
and when I lay in bed-----
it's spinning around,
like a little child-----
running wild-----
in a dream-----
in a dream-----
in a dream-----
in a dream-----

All things must pass-----all things must end-----
like the stars, and moonlight-----

They always seem to fade / before they disappear
as the day begins------
needles and pins-----
a knife in my back,
pull it on through-----
I'll bleed for you-----
cherry red-----
cherry red-----
cherry red-----
cherry red-----

I wish that you-----could understand-----
just how, you made me feel-----

Each and every time / that you'd fly away
like a frightened dove-----
when I mentioned love-----
it's always there,

in your eyes-----
the warm sunrise-----
melting me-----
melting me-----
melting me-----
melting me-----

Now every now and then-----I hear your name-----
I think of love, I think of pain-----

The two have become / ever so entwined
like the rose and thorn-----
since my heart was torn-----
a leaf from a tree,
falls to the ground-----
the devil's sound-----
inside of me-----
inside of me-----
inside of me-----
inside of me-----

The Thanator

The Thanator screams, flying high,
wings silhouetted against the sky.
Dark against light, colors make sound.
Falling at random, they hit the ground.
Uniquely bright, the fire unfolds.
Shadows at night, what future holds
the bird of paradise, found and then lost.
Upon its steel chest, a poem embossed.

Just like white birds want to sing all day,
and the blue bird, she cries.
Red birds go to heaven, babe,
and the black bird just dies.
The black bird just dies-----
the black bird dies-----
And I'm a black bird, babe-----
I'm a black bird, babe----
Yes, I'm a black bird, babe;
and I'm dying just for you-----

With a Knife

Down,
down,
down
on
Los Angeles Street.
Millions of people dead on their feet;
starving for love, starving for life.
If you've got some to spare,
they'll take it with a knife.

And just around the corner
in the Hollywood hills,
people who can only get thrills
from burning up hundred dollar bills.
What money buys......
what money kills!

You may not like the Santa Fe way,
but I'd take their town any old day
over the smog filled minds
of smoky L.A.

The Virgin Dreamer

......the smoke brings emotion.

The hours, they separate us;
the logistics of a struggle,
the quotient of love,
a tragic irony,
a turn towards availability.

I seek a mind that soars;
I must move on to harmonious freedom

Do you trust me?

A casket of death
with each passing.
Neptune rises;
the blue joker moves freely,
not a slave to one suit,
high
or
low.

Go ahead,
ask yourself, what is your most valuable possession?

Your love?
Your soul?

......your lover's soul?

The queen of diamonds......with the blue joker.
(a Pair)
unnatural, yet pure.
Come with me and don't be afraid.
Believe in me,

don't be afraid;
discard all you mirrors.
Do not see yourself (for sometime);
you too, can be a blue joker.

Do you trust me?

Innumerable snakes (hiss);
the swords of passion pierce your heart (kiss).
Do you want my soul?
Come and get me;
follow the rise, and fall, and rise;
the wind, the sun, the sand,
all at your service.

Not only is it the end of time,
but it is the end of weather.
The severe intensity of it all;
another smoldering love.
In my head, a lit stick of dynamite;
out of my mind,
then......
out of my sight.

The virgin dreamer
seeks a mind that soars;
and must move on to harmonious freedom.

Do you trust me?

Do you think it will be different this time,
knowing what you're knowing,
knowing where you're going?
There is no more magic,
only a futile effort.

Poor Boy

I said,
I hate going to bed,
terminus death......symbolical sleep
She said,
I don't know what you mean,
your thoughts are too deep,
and you incorrectly spelled the word, terminus.

I said,
I'm whacked out in the head,
but I am not insane.
She said,
I know you are,
but I am tired of hearing you complain.

He was a poor boy
and she was society getting high.
He never did expect much,
just thought he'd give it a try.

Gave his all, and ten times more.
Made a big scream and shout,
but no matter what he did,
it could never work out.

He lost his heart,
he lost his mind,
and he lost his will......
for humankind

Now every time he opens his eyes,
he falls flat on his face;
a simple story, a simple rule.
A poor boy put in his place.

Without Hesitation

A jungle is a jungle and a city is a scheme;
take away the world, and take away a dream.
When your time has come, you go sailing down that stream
back to the jungle, where you're sleeping in your dream.
I miss you so very much,
out here......there is no loving touch.

I think about you at night with death in my eye.
I miss you so very much, as the stars would miss the sky.
I wish you would have run with me,
but you couldn't leave your friends and family.
I think of all the promise we'd find,
never concerning, what was left behind.

Sour grapes and broken bottles of wine;
your life is more important than mine.
Although it hurts dearly, I have to go,
across the effervescent plateau.
It all seems like a simple jerk, or twist of fate,
but somehow......in the back of my mind
I feel like I may never see you again.
Another vase full of dead flowers
and somehow......I am happy.

Aladdin hides around the corner with three wishes.
The first was the best, I gave away the rest.
You look at me, I look at you;
eyes upon heart, heart split in two.
If you want to know how many times
this can happen without devastation.
Then, I can tell you this is the last time,
without hesitation.

Out of the Swamp

Summer's song,
I sang too long;
a lock upon my wheel.
It went too fast,
it couldn't last;
a melted heart of steel.

Behind every knife, a starving wife
hungry for some love.
There's no need to talk, I'm a hunting hawk
searching for a dove.

Remember the 'Song of Escapades',
when I dwelled in the Everglades;
the beauty is the story.
He came out of the swamp
playing 'Bron-Y-Aur Stomp';
the rest is quite gory.

A young lady is waiting,
the dragon is hating
everything that stands in its way.
She never heard it coming,
the drummer was drumming;
the beat of the final day

One lash of his tail,
and she began to wail;
out popped both eyes.
Her brain was unloading,
her breast still exploding;
yet she offered up her thighs.

The Brightest Stars

Without the bad times, time would be obsolete;
only the end is written in concrete.

Do you think you can save me from eternal madness?
Do you think you can save me, Sister Sadness?

Denounce the perils of fortuitous fame;
another forgotten monster of shame.

Angels of passion, they tell the virgin's story,
and at 3:00am heaven is bursting with glory.

Lambent girl perched on the corner;
everyone passes by, I had to warn her

of the deep fathom blue daffodil,
standing alone at the top of the hill

looking over the lake where serpents swim.
The brightest stars will eventually turn dim.

Pirate Lunacy

The medicine man, he demonstrates,
what it is like to hold aces and eights.
The gunslinger, he is his own healer,
when he fires his guns at the dealer.

I know every situation must unfold,
according to the cards that you hold.
Stumble into romance saloon, find your accuser,
you will always come out......the loser

Shotgun blast, another jealous lover.
Everybody run for cover,
way back inside your brain;
for every ounce of pleasure, there's a ton of pain.

Suicide wheels, they're just rolling along;
just one blowout and you're gone, gone, gone.
Took the passion flight heading straight for the sun;
lips wrapped around the barrel of a gun.

I am sure you could probably guess,
how his life turned out to be such a mess.
Yes, they put on their armor like drones;
black skies fill with stones.

He liked the kitten, he hated the cat;
it always seems to turn out like that.
Storm clouds, they move in fast;
a good thing can never last.

Another man and woman divide,
so convinced that they tried
to sing, sing, the sparrow's song
all of the day, and all night long.

They said their goodbyes;
told each other lies.
I love you, I love you.
I'll miss you, I'll miss you.
Goodbye, goodbye.

I wish I could go back and do it all over again,
but then, but then, where would I be when......
I miss you?

For a love that is born
is sure......sure to be torn,
like the tornado and the hurricane
always bring us pain, pain, pain.

He was lonely, she was scared,
but neither of them ever dared
to tell the other just what they were thinking,
so they just kept on sinking,
and sinking,
and sinking,
until they hit the bottom of the deepest blue.
knowing now, that dreams don't come true.
I should have known, normal life would break down;
pirate lunacy, sailing from town to town.

Thomas Walker

Springtime in the Mourning Mountains

Staring out my broken window
looking at the morning snow;
suitcase in my brain,
but I've got nowhere to go.

Life is beholden to despair
when there's no one for to care.
Oh, I wish you'd come out to play,
little snowshoe hare.

It is so sad when you have to depend
on the thoughts that you send;
to be your one and only lover,
to be your one and only friend.

This old, ghosted silver mine
has got me missing the divine
girl that I used to know;
even though she left me cryin'.

She'll say I am better off out here,
then, she'll say I love you dear.
It doesn't matter what I want
until the blizzard is clear.

Love melts down like ice,
but cool water is still nice.
You can't always have the best,
sometimes you must sacrifice.

I guess I'll keep going on my own
until the flesh rips from the bone.
Hurting is the beckoned norm,
when you're desperately alone.

How about one more time for good measure;
try to find that sunken treasure.
No, it is best we're on our way
to some new enlightened pleasure.

And now that I'm down to just one pawn,
I watch the water disappear at dawn,
into the vast and open sea.
Another winter is gone.

These mourning mountains are so steep,
and thus, the river runs through deep.
The final night, listlessly falling;
I thank you for eternal sleep.

I'll see you again tomorrow,
when it's time to beg and borrow;
watching the morning's icy rain
through my broken window of sorrow.

Delicate Geometry

Reflections of serenities,
written in the autumn breeze,
brings a goddess to her knees
just for me,
just for me.

Unmerciful maiden
you petrify my life
with your phallus insanity.
Cubical heirloom of the enchantress;
my spite alone will keep me moving on.

In this slot machine world
everyone has a chance, I think.
Cannibal glory, you know where she's been;
it only takes one second to win.

Light another joss stick,
and you better make it quick
because losing can last a lifetime
in the land of forgotten lipstick.

We all have some sort of obsession.
Let this be the first lesson
in some new insipid evolution.
Geishas are on the way;
a combination of natural things.
I must work my way through
the delicate geometry.
I might not be back for a month or two.

I Howl for You (a coyote prayer)

The desert roamer, a life without friends,
on a continuous hunt, he never depends
on anyone or anything to guide him through;
he'll keep on searching, until he finds you.
He always gets into trouble, but gets right back out,
he growls at his mistakes, but he'll never pout,
he howls at the moon but not too loud,
he howls to be heard but hides from the crowd.
The sly and cunning will never fade, for what it's worth;
the coyote will be, the last mammal on earth.

Mutiny Anticipation

We'll go forward.
I'll see you hang,
in the captain's quarters
(he knew that his men were plotting his death);
he read it in the twists and turns of the stars.
The night was foul.
Awkwardly, we support the leaders
but the time comes when a dreamer's soul
must resist.
A cult is a cult
in every walk of life,
like birds in a flock;
a student, branded by a university
must be slaughtered for food.
We are all invisibly closer to our destiny;
look to the black horizon
and feel the motion......in your heart.
The captain savors 'the discovery'.
Whoso is the adventurer, the dreamer,
whoso has accepted authority;
the constant sound of waves flowing,
flowing blood through the veins.
I was born on an outlying island
where one doubts his ability,
but now I'm on the other side of the world;
my face burns from the cool winter breeze.
We'll go forward.
I'll see you drown
in the captain's quarters
(he knew that his men were plotting his death);
the eyelid opens, and casts
a blanket of gold across the sea,
an immortal half circle
lifting above the water.
We are the lowliest.

Our success lies in our failures......
our mightiest failures;
the sadness of a violent expedition.
Back home, naked people emerge
by the fireside and cry on their mother's lap;
my emotions have been swindled.
I stand behind my actions
but am tired......
painfully tired.
Yet, I am not oblivious to our goal......
copulation and devastation.
We'll go forward.
I'll see you bleed
in the captain's quarters
(he knew that his men were plotting his death);
the rain is coming down like broken glass.
A last glimpse of steel;
this bullet bears your name.
We hereby take full possession of this voyage;
the red pool of repetition
fills the captain's quarters.
On his desk a childlike note,
"I won't hurt you......"
The trust had gone, the clouds had shifted;
dancing rainbows fill the air.
A distant voice from above,
'I see land, beautiful, beautiful......land.'
Now let us be placed
among the exalted men in history,
"......I wonder if you can begin
to understand the pain of neglect?"

Warm Sand

Delicate beauty,
you are still so young,
and now that you are rid of me;
erotic sandstorms blowing free.

With nothing to love,
there is nothing to live…..for;
find yourself in the warm crystal sands,
let it filter through your hands.

Fight for your passion
with intrinsic glory;
the shadow breaks across the dune,
emancipation makes us so immune.

In the City

When you are lost
in the city
and you haven't got
a dollar to spend,
just hold out your hands;
there is always
someone there to lend......
you a look of disgust,
and someone to spit
in your face,
saying, "I wish
they would ban
the poor
from the human race."
Get in your car,
and go home
to charge your batteries
for the next day.
I am glad for
all those satisfied,
but I'd best be
on my way.

Thomas Walker

Mississippi Queen

He fell in love
on the Mississippi River.
He said he'd give her
his life,
but everyone knows
how the river overflows;
cutting through like a knife
When push came to shove
she ran like the mouse,
away from the farmer's wife.

It is so easy to love you
you're so soft inside.
Open up the flood gates,
let us decide.

She was right in her world,
he was wrong is his.
She said, 'I just wasn't meant for you.'
He said, 'Well then, what is?'

Temporary Direction

A jungle in the sea,
growing in front of me.
Another promise,
generosity;
floating,
abandoned felicity.
The early morning sun,
provides a
temporary direction
for anyone.
I have been up all night
sitting here
on my windowsill.
Contemplating how,
I would like to kill,
the butterfly
flittering by.
It makes me think of you,
but with the half turn
of an instance,
I soon realize
that sex is in the lips,
love is in the eyes.

Driving to the Woods

Mr. Raccoon,
it is such a beautiful day.
Mr. Raccoon,
won't you come out to play?
You are so lonely,
but then again, free.
Won't you come out
to play with me......
just for a while?

It is so hard
to keep from being sad;
with the good times,
there is always bad.
The good news is
I'm still alive.
The bad news is,
it's a long, long drive......
just to see you smile.

The Vacancy

Tangerine eye lines as far as I can see;
pretty girls hanging from a tree.
My angel, a nubile milky renaissance;
reckless shade of indigo, a liquid nuance.

Stranded lovers in auburn fields of ecstasy;
violent stormy episodes of jealousy.
Picture perfect
fuchsia life (inside of her);
stoic silence
of gentle hands,
and then she begins to purr
for me.

Golden cattails growing,
blowing......beside the lake.
In the water, they see
reflections of a snake.

Open up the sunlight,
captivating a wicked soul.
Underwater journey,
(harpooning) Amphitrite is the goal.
Cavernous beauty
stay close, you could get lost;
exploding visions
now your name is embossed......
on the steel graveyards
of my memory.
Off to the left,
a vacancy
where you were
always meant to be.

The Beginning

The end is the beginning
of all great things;
with violins playing
long before the trumpets.
When one plus one
equals the caterpillar,
and finality frees
the butterfly.
In youth, there is
a hopeless abandon.
In death, there is
a great knowledge
of survival.
The wonder of inspiration
lies in the valley
not the peak.
Born in the ancient
memory of time,
where all the children
stand in line;
waiting for
the evening train
waiting for
the winter rain.
The rain grows to the sea;
the end of calamity,
you, and me.

About the Author

Born and raised in St. Petersburg, Florida, Thomas Walker left a promising career with an international architecture firm for the adventures of Alaska. He has been living in Eagle River, Alaska since 1999 and is forever afflicted with the disease so greatly known as poetry. Thomas Walker has a previously published book of poetry, *Ashes In My Skull*, and many more in the works.

Thomas Walker Publications

Eagle River, Alaska

www.ingramcontent.com/pod-product-compliance
Lightning Source LLC
Chambersburg PA
CBHW061148040426
42445CB00013B/1604